Blake's G

INVESTING
in
SHARES

GW01398050

Linda Fischer

PASCAL
PRESS

Copyright © Pascal Press 2003
Reprinted 2004
ISBN 1 877085 23 5

Pascal Press
PO Box 250
Glebe NSW 2037
(02) 8585 4044
www.pascalpress.com.au

Publisher: Vivienne Petris Joannou
Series editors: Emma Driver and Ian Rohr
Editor: Emma Driver
Design, page layout and cover by *DiZign* Pty Ltd
Photos by Comstock, Ingram Publishing, Eyewire and PhotoDisc
Printed in Australia by Printing Creations

A NOTE FROM THE PUBLISHER

We make a lot of crucial decisions about our taxation, legal and investment issues with very little comprehensible information at hand. We are often dealing with people like lawyers, accountants and real estate agents who know a lot about these topics. This puts the average person at a big disadvantage, and can lead to you getting the worse end of the deal.

That is why I decided to extend the Go Guide series into the areas of tax, law and investment. I wanted to provide people with enough information to be able to at least ask the right questions and to avoid the pitfalls that are so easy to fall into.

As readers of the previous Blake's Go Guides on computer topics will know, our goal is to break through the information overload and provide you with only the really useful material that you will need in every day life.

If you have any comments or ideas on how these books could be improved further then please don't hesitate to email me at matthew@pascalpress.com.au.

Matthew Blake
Publisher

ABOUT THE AUTHOR

Linda Fischer is a financial and corporate writer and researcher with over 10 years' experience in the financial and investment fields, having worked with the Australian Stock Exchange, TD Waterhouse Investor Services and E*Trade Australia. She has been a researcher on the television program *The Money Show* (Nine Network) and has been a contributing writer to several well-regarded books on investment.

TABLE OF CONTENTS

INTRODUCTION

Around 40% of all Australian adults currently have a stake in the Australian share market. In effect, they are **part-owners** of companies. Over recent years, share ownership has soared, partly as a result of prominent **'floats'** including Telstra, QANTAS, the Commonwealth Bank and the TAB. More Australians have joined the share holding ranks through the **demutualisation** of AMP and NRMA, and others through **employee share ownership plans**. Many more own shares via their superannuation fund – and they may not even be aware of it. And then, of course, there are the thousands of investors actively buying and selling shares 'on the market' on a daily basis.

The fact that Australia has one of the highest per capita rates of share ownership in the world adds weight to the observation that the share market is **accessible to all levels of investor** – from the average person in the street to high-stakes traders. The stock market isn't forbidding alien terrain and the fundamental recipe for buying and selling shares is not a closely guarded secret. Essentially, the stock market is an **actual 'marketplace'** governed by the laws of supply and demand. It moves in cycles, so it is possible to pick up affordable shares which can then be sold at a profit a few years down the track.

Having said that, investing in shares is by no means a 'sure thing' and even the professionals can get it wrong. However, knowledge is power and an **informed investment strategy** guided by thorough research and/or expert advice can help you to minimise the risks and maximise your returns. To become a smart investor you should, firstly:

- establish your **investment goals**
- understand your **risk profile**
- mobilise a **plan of action** – and then stick to it.

Armed with the knowledge that the market experiences **peaks and troughs**, you can stay on track by building a diversified portfolio of stocks in good quality companies that will generally grow in value over the long term. To achieve this, it is important to first develop a fundamental understanding of:

- the **stock market**
- **share analysis**
- some basic **investment rules**.

WHY INVEST IN SHARES?

So, what drives people to invest in the share market? The reason is usually to 'grow their money' in order to **achieve their financial goals**.

There are four **investment asset classes**, which are:

◆ shares
◆ property
◆ cash
◆ fixed income.

While **shares** carry the **highest risk** in the short term, over a period of time they tend to give investors the **highest return** on initial investment outlay. If you stay in the market for seven to ten years and ride out the share market's inevitable fluctuations they will, as a rule, deliver greater returns than the other asset classes. Shares are recognised as a **tax-effective** investment and can be expected to **beat inflation**.

As a guide, between 1985 and 2001, Australian shares returned around 13.9% and international shares returned 15.4%. On the other hand, bank bills returned 9.4%, while listed property trusts returned 12.3%. However, if you glance at the table on the following page, you'll notice that the returns on shares – both Australian and international – tend to fluctuate quite dramatically. In 1986, Australian shares recorded a massive 52.2% rise, but four years later they posted a loss of –17.5%. In those same two years (1986 and 1990), bank bills returned 16.9% and 15.1% respectively. This is a good example of the 'risk = reward' axiom and why the **time frame of your investment**, rather than **the time of your entry point into the market**, is the key to a successful investment strategy.

The table on the following page shows the relative performance of the different classes of assets from 1985–2001.

ASSET CLASS RETURNS, 1985–2001

Note: Returns of over 20% are highlighted in blue; negative returns are in red.

	Bank bills	AEQ	AFI	IEQ	IFI	LPT
1985	15.0%	44.1%	8.1%	70.8%	25.0%	5.3%
1986	16.9%	52.2%	18.9%	45.4%	25.6%	35.4%
1987	14.9%	−7.9%	18.6%	7.1%	13.5%	5.8%
1988	12.1%	17.9%	9.1%	4.0%	13.8%	16.1%
1989	17.3%	17.4%	14.4%	26.3%	18.0%	2.4%
1990	15.1%	−17.5%	19.0%	−15.1%	13.3%	8.7%
1991	10.7%	34.2%	24.7%	20.0%	18.4%	20.1%
1992	6.8%	−2.3%	10.4%	4.9%	11.1%	7.0%
1993	5.4%	45.4%	16.3%	23.8%	14.8%	30.1%
1994	5.4%	−8.7%	−4.7%	−8.1%	−2.6%	−5.6%
1995	7.8%	20.2%	18.6%	26.0%	20.1%	12.7%
1996	7.3%	14.6%	11.8%	6.2%	10.7%	14.6%
1997	5.5%	12.2%	12.2%	41.6%	10.4%	20.3%
1998	5.1%	11.6%	9.5%	32.3%	10.4%	18.0%
1999	5.0%	16.1%	−1.2%	17.2%	0.9%	−6.2%
2000	6.3%	3.6%	12.1%	2.2%	10.1%	18.1%
2001	5.2%	10.1%	5.4%	−10.0%	7.4%	15.1%
Annualised return	9.4%	13.9%	11.7%	15.4%	12.8%	12.3%

Source: Fiducian Portfolio Services
For figures for 2002 onwards please contact your financial advisor or stockbroker.

- AEQ (Australian Equities): S&P/ASX All Ordinaries Index
- IEQ (International Equities): MSCI ex-Aust ($A)
- LPT (Listed Property Trusts): S&P/ASX 500 Property Trusts Index
- AFI (Australian Fixed Interest): UBSWA Composite Bond Index
- IFI (International Fixed Interest): SSB World Hedged Bond Index
- Bank bills: UBSWA Bank Bill Index

CHOOSING YOUR SHARES

What is a share?

Shares represent **part-ownership** or **equity** in a company listed on the **Australian Stock Exchange (ASX)**. When a company is listed on the ASX it means that it has been **'floated'** as a public company and its shares are traded on the market. Floats, or **Initial Public Offers (IPOs)** are discussed in more detail on page 35. As a shareholder, you effectively have a stake in the management of the company and you have bought the right to attend **Annual General Meetings (AGMs)** and rub shoulders with the big end of town. Notionally, you have a say in the running of the company. However, for many smaller investors, the last point is academic. If they are unhappy with the company's performance they tend to show their dissatisfaction by offloading their shares rather than grilling the Board at the AGM.

Shareholders may be entitled to a share of a company's profit through the payment of **dividends**, as well as reaping the benefits of an increase in the **market value of the stock**. On the other hand, companies don't always record profits, in which case the value of your shares could decline – sometimes dramatically.

Types of shares

Ordinary shares

The bulk of shares in most Australian investors' portfolios tend to be **ordinary shares**. Shares are generally described as **ordinary** if they are **fully paid**, meaning that you have total ownership of the share, with no residual payments owing to the issuer.

Contributing or partly paid shares

Contributing (partly paid) shares are a less common type of share. They differ from ordinary shares in the sense that they **are not fully paid** and the investor will be required to make further payments to the issuer at a future date. Telstra 'Mark 2' was a high profile example where the second instalment wasn't payable for quite some time after the float. Typically, the greater the proportion paid up on the share, the higher the dividend payment for the shareholder. These types of shares can be sold on the ASX prior to full payment.

Preference shares

Unlike ordinary shares, **preference shares** tend to pay a **fixed rate of return or dividend**. As the name suggests, owners of preference shares receive preferential treatment over ordinary shareholders and they are at the head of the queue when dividends are paid out. They are also given **preferential access** (over ordinary shareholders) to remaining capital should the company collapse. However, in an interesting twist, the **voting rights** of preference shareholders aren't on equal footing with those of ordinary shareholders.

Preference shareholders will generally receive a dividend that **exceeds** that paid to ordinary shareholders if the company is not turning as big a profit as expected. On the flip side, preference shares can also have a **drawback**. A fixed dividend can be extremely limiting if a company has recorded a stronger than expected performance. In this situation, ordinary shareholders can potentially earn higher dividends than preference shareholders.

Selecting shares

The share market also provides **plenty of choices** to suit a wide range of Australian investors. You can buy shares in well over a thousand companies listed on the Australian Stock Exchange (ASX) across 24 major sectors. The companies can be:

- ◆ **Blue chip companies**. These are large, established, well-managed companies with a solid track record and profitability over a long period. They are spread across a range of sectors and 'old economy' stocks feature prominently.
- ◆ **Medium-sized (mid-cap) companies**. These are often in the technology and services sectors and at times their growth rate may exceed that of more established companies. While the rewards can be higher than blue chips, they usually carry more risk because they are still developing.
- ◆ **Speculative companies**. These tend to be smaller and younger. Many examples can be found in the technology and mining sectors. Often a major increase in their share value will depend on a significant discovery or innovation. This element of the 'unknown' makes them a higher risk investment and they are also more prone to failure.

As a rule, investment advisors concur that the key to success is to purchase quality stocks across a **diverse range of companies** in a **number of sectors** (a 'sector' refers to a **group of securities sharing common factors, such as the Telecommunications sector or Banking and Finance sector**). Potential investors should also be aware of the fact that major declines in the value of share prices may occur in some years, meaning that the value of your investments will also drop (see table

on page 8). However, it is widely recognised that the value of shares in **good, quality companies** (see page 28) have shown a tendency to **stage a comeback** in the long term.

By becoming a shareholder you have the opportunity to profit from your investment in two basic ways – through **growth** and through **income**.

◆ **Growth shares** offer the potential for **capital gains** over time.
◆ **Income shares** provide the possibility of rewarding payments in the form of **dividends**.

Capital growth

When the price of a share you have bought **increases in value**, you are making money by way of **capital growth**. A capital gain occurs when your shares are sold for more money than you initially paid for them. For example, imagine you have a shareholding of **$1.00 per share**.

◆ **Capital gain**: If the shares trade on the market at **$2.00**, you've made a capital gain of $1.00 per share, and the value of your share parcel has doubled.
◆ **Unrealised capital gain**: If you decide to hold onto the shares, your capital gain is **unrealised**, but the **paper value** of your shares has increased.
◆ **Loss**: If the price of each share dips to 50 cents you will **lose 50%** of your investment.

Significant capital gains are usually realised over the **longer term**, keeping in mind that share prices tend to rise and fall, and that sometimes these **fluctuations** have a sudden and significant impact on share prices. Share value can increase or decline based on several factors, including the company's future earnings prospects, its current performance in comparison to its competitors in the marketplace and the health of the economy.

Income (dividends)

The other way to make money from shares is through **dividends**. These are the payments made by a company to its shareholders (those who have bought shares in the company). In effect, dividends represent your share of the company's after-tax profit and they are typically paid **twice a year**. Not all dividends are created equal – the amount of your dividend depends on the number of shares that you own and the size of the company's profit.

Some companies issue **franked dividends** to shareholders, which means that the **company tax has already been paid** on them. They can be **fully franked**, or **partly franked** to a certain proportion. The benefit of franked dividends is that the portion of tax already paid by the company on the dividends you earned can be used to **offset your tax liability**.

Some companies give shareholders the opportunity to acquire extra shares via a **dividend reinvestment plan** instead of receiving a dividend cheque.

It's also important to note that **not all companies pay dividends**. Some channel a high proportion of their profits back into building the business and pay their investors low (or no) dividends. Information about a company's dividend policy and whether it pays franked or unfranked dividends can be found in company reports. Finally, **shareholders are never guaranteed of a dividend**. If company fortunes and profits are down, investors may miss out.

Dividend imputation

The dividend imputation system works by giving investors in Australian companies paying the corporate tax rate (30 cents in the dollar) **credit** for tax paid on company profits. This credit can be offset against the tax payable on your dividend and the tax payable on other income if your marginal tax rate is lower than the company rate. In effect, how much you benefit from dividend imputation depends on your marginal tax rate. **Excess franking credits** on your tax return could end up as a tax refund. In some cases, dividends can be **tax-free** because the tax rebate is equal to the amount of company tax paid, for example, if your tax rate is 30 cents, or less, in the dollar. If you are paying the highest marginal tax rate of **48.5%** and your shares are fully franked, you will only have to pay enough tax to make up the difference between your marginal rate and the corporate tax rate of 30 cents.

Prior to the introduction of dividend imputation in 1987, dividends were hit by a **'double tax'** because companies paid dividends from their profits after paying the corporate tax on their income. Shareholders would then have to take their turn and also pay tax on the dividend. Dividend imputation has thus helped to make shares more attractive from a tax perspective.

Other benefits

Besides the prospects of higher returns over the long term in comparison to other investments, shares also offer investors other **benefits** including:

Convenience

Unlike other many other asset classes, the money invested in shares is **easily redeemable**. For example, your funds aren't locked away in the same way as fixed income investments like term deposits. They also offer the added convenience of allowing you to sell just a **part** of your share

portfolio. This is a clear advantage over investments like property – for obvious reasons, selling off part of a house is generally not an option!

Buying and selling shares is also a **relatively simple and quick** process, and brokerage fees are very cost-effective. On the other hand, property transactions are time-consuming (often stretching into months) and attract hefty fees (in the thousands of dollars).

Shares also have a high level of **liquidity** which means that they can be **turned back into cash quickly** – unlike property, which can take a long time to sell. Therefore, shares give you relatively **easy access** to your money.

Bonus shares

Some companies also issue **bonus shares** to their existing shareholders at no cost. Essentially it's a 'gift' to all shareholders and another way of handing over a part of the profits to investors. The number of shares that you – and all other shareholders – receive is proportionate to the size of your current shareholding. Because the size of everyone's share parcel increases, there is no corresponding increase in the proportion of the company owned as a result of the bonus issue.

Also, **capital growth of the bonus shares can't be realised** straight away as the change to the value of the shareholding is not instantaneous and the overall value of your shareholding at that time remains the same until the market value increases.

Rights issues

Rights issues provide shareholders with the right, but not the obligation, to buy more shares in the company at a **lower price** than the current market value. A rights issue is usually offered to existing shareholders as a means of **raising capital** for the company and as an added incentive no brokerage is charged. The number of new shares available to an investor is determined by the size of his or her **existing shareholding** – the more shares you already own, the more you are invited to buy in the rights issue.

Rights issues can take one of two **forms**:

- a **renounceable rights issue** can be sold off on the market allowing another investor to acquire the right to that issue if the original shareholder decides not to take up the offer.
- a **non-renounceable rights issue** will terminate if the issue isn't accepted by the shareholder by a specified date and cannot be sold or traded by the shareholder or the issuing company.

ARE SHARES THE RIGHT INVESTMENT FOR YOU?

So, how do you know if shares are the right investment for you? Before taking the plunge into the share market, it's vitally important to **define and set your investment goals**. As a rule, investment professionals recommend that you should:

- assess your current **financial position**
- evaluate your **attitude to risk**
- work out your **investor temperament** in order to develop the most appropriate investment strategy.

Risk profile

In the investment world, the much-chanted mantra is **risk equals return**. Quite simply, it means the **more risk** you are willing to take, the **higher your returns** are likely to be.

How much investment risk you can tolerate is the defining feature of your **risk profile**. Risk profiles range from the **cautious** (play it safe, low-risk) to the **very aggressive** (take a huge chance, high-risk). The key to managing investment risk is to assess how much you can tolerate given your **personal and financial circumstances**.

Degrees of risk

It is possible to protect your money by taking a relatively **cautious investment strategy**. For example, **term deposits** maintain a stable value and pose **less short-term risk**. Investing in the more **volatile** asset classes means you will be taking on **more short-term risk**. If you're investing for the **long term**, however, higher risk investments such as shares or listed property will have a better chance of outpacing inflation and providing a **higher return**.

Some important **factors** to consider before investing are your age, income level, job security, ongoing earning opportunities, investment goals and timeframes, and your investor temperament. Most advisors also point out that your **level of risk tolerance** will probably **change** over time as you move through different life stages. Generally, with age comes more responsibility – and possibly fewer earning opportunities.

Risk profiles can be seen as occupying rungs on a **'risk/return' ladder**. The higher you climb, the greater the level of risk and the greater your potential investment returns. However, it also means that you have further to fall and more chance of losing a portion of your investment capital.

Upper rungs

Younger investors or **high-income earners** are more likely to head towards the top or high-risk end of the risk/reward ladder. They are more likely to be attracted to the greater and faster potential returns offered by the share market. They would probably be less inclined to lock away a lot of money for the long term in fixed-income investments with lower returns. They may also have their portfolio weighted towards higher risk shares and markets such as the technology sector, growth companies, smaller companies and emerging international markets.

Middle rungs

As people start families or approach **middle age**, they might become more **cautious** and move towards the middle of the risk/return ladder. At this stage of life an investment in a combination of **medium and high-risk investments** like investment property, listed property trusts, an international share fund or Australian blue chip shares might look like a more attractive option.

Lower rungs

People with heavy financial commitments, facing uncertain job prospects or approaching retirement are likely to have a **lower risk tolerance**. They typically sit on the lower rungs of the risk ladder and might be willing to sacrifice the prospect of higher returns for investments in 'safer' assets, with less exposure to high-risk investments like shares. Investors fitting this risk profile are more likely to view the biggest risk as the possible loss of a large chunk of their money that could be difficult to recoup. Consequently, they are more likely to opt for cash management trusts, term deposits or fixed-interest securities such as bonds.

Investors fitting all these profiles could also explore the option of investing in a **managed share fund** which offers a large selection of funds with various rates of risk and. Managed share funds are covered on pages 53-55.

Investor temperament

Finally, your **investor temperament** is based on **how much risk** you are prepared to take, based on emotional factors. Some investors have nerves of steel and like to 'live on the edge', and they accept higher levels of risk as the trade-off for higher returns. Others have sleepless nights over the thought of losing their money and take the safer, low-risk investment path. Evaluating your investor temperament is an important step in deciding whether shares – or what type of shares – are right for you.

WHAT IS THE STOCK MARKET?

As the name suggests, the stock market is actually a **'marketplace'** where investors and traders meet – although not in a physical sense – to **buy and sell shares.** Stock exchanges provide the facilities to enable share transactions to take place on companies 'listed' with that exchange. In Australia, the stock market was formed in 1987 by linking the six State exchanges to operate as a national marketplace – the **Australian Stock Exchange (ASX)**. Since 1990, buying and selling has moved from the trading floor to the computer, and share transactions are now conducted via the **Stock Exchange Automated Trading System (SEATS)**.

The share market operates like many other markets that sell goods, and the prices of those goods are shaped largely by **supply and demand**. Share prices will receive a welcome boost if there is a strong demand from buyers in the market, but will go down if there is a lack of investor demand.

Indices

The Australian share market is home to several **indices** (plural of 'index') including the **All Ordinaries** (often called the 'All Ords') and the **ASX S&P 50**, **100**, **200** and **300** which are calculated by the US credit rating agency **Standard & Poor's** (often referred to as 'S&P').

Groups of shares are combined in **indices** to provide the means for monitoring movements in various markets around the globe over a period of time. This lets investors see the market as a whole at a glance by providing **benchmarks**. When the **media** reports on the direction of the share market, the commentators sum up movements in specific indices, as well as mentioning the performance of individual shares – usually the big movers on a given day that impact on a particular index.

Some of the **well-known indices** around the world include:

- the **Dow Jones** index, based on the average share price of major companies in the **USA**
- the **FTSE** index in London, based on the average share price of major companies in the **UK**
- the US-based **NASDAQ**, which is comprised only of **technology-related stocks.**

You will probably be familiar with the **All Ordinaries** through stock market bulletins on the evening news. It is the most commonly quoted Australian market index. It is made up of the most actively traded companies and is responsible for the **greatest percentage of share turnover**. The index provides a **broad measurement** of the total performance of the Australian market and comprises the majority of listed companies trading on the ASX.

RESEARCHING YOUR OPTIONS

It's almost impossible to overstate the importance of **carefully doing your research** before you even think about placing your first trade on the market. Good research is an important and ongoing component of profitable investing. The more informed you are, the better your chances of making good decisions and realising **steady returns** on your investment. There is an abundance of information available to investors. Some useful and easily accessible research tools are listed below.

Financial media

The different **financial media** offer a wide range of affordable information on issues that impact on the Australian and international share markets.

Newspapers

The major **national newspapers** are a great affordable and accessible reference point for topical share market information. They generally contain specialised business pages and most provide **share market summaries** and **share tables** (see pages 38-39) in the Finance section. Major dailies cover financial issues that impact on the share market in their general news sections. Most weekend papers also offer finance and investment supplements. The *Australian Financial Review* is an influential national paper that provides authoritative commentary on corporate news, the economy, local and global markets and a wide range of investment issues. It is staple reading for informed investors and market professionals.

Magazines

Three useful Australian publications are *Shares*, *Personal Investor* and *Money Magazine*. These monthly magazines provide extensive information pitched at various levels of investment expertise. They include useful articles on issues that influence the share market, companies, industry profiles, broad economic commentary and interviews with key market players. However, with the thousands of shares trading on the market, the newspapers and magazines can't provide constant coverage on them all.

Radio and television

Radio and television provide daily **stock market bulletins** during the news broadcasts and also cover stories affecting the market, such as interest rate movements, business and consumer confidence, unemployment and balance of trade figures. For a price you can also access **specialist cable TV business channels** like CNN, CNBC (Australia) and Bloomberg. Business information services like Reuters (www.reuters.com) and AAP's *Marketi* (aap.com.au/marketi) are also worth a look.

Internet sites

The Internet offers a seemingly endless supply of share market information such as current financial news, stock quotes, topical investment articles, advice, opinions and analysis tools. Many of them are free to access. Some of the most popular are listed here.

Australian Business Research www.abr.com.au	Huntleys' Online (investment services and business information) www.huntley.com.au
Australian Financial Review www.afr.com.au	InvestorWeb www.investorweb.com.au
Australian Financial Services Directory www.afsd.com.au	MoneyManager www.moneymanager.com.au
The Australian Investor www.australianinvestor.com.au	My Money www.mymoney.com.au
Australian Securities and Investments Commission Financial Tips & Safety www.fido.asic.gov.au	NineMSN's Money site www.ninemsn.com.au/money
The Australian Stock Exchange www.asx.com.au	Shares & Personal Investor www.personalinvestor.com.au
Egoli (SHAW Stockbroking) www.egoli.com.au	The Sydney Morning Herald (Business section) www.smh.com.au/business
EquityCafé www.equitycafe.com.au	Telstra's Money site www.money.bigpond.com
Financial Planning Association of Australia www.fpa.asn.au	TradingRoom www.tradingroom.com.au
HotCopper Australia www.hotcopper.com.au	

Most **listed companies** also have their own **websites** and these can be good sources of information about the company's activities.

You can find share prices, analysis, newsletters, ASX announcements and reports on **individual broker websites**. Usually, however, you will require a password and log-on for live quotes and 'member only' services.

Courses

The ASX offers a range of **share market courses and seminars** to suit all levels of investor, from the novice to the more experienced investor. Free and paid **on-line interactive tutorials** are also on offer. Simply register your details at www.asx.com.au/education/courses_showcase.shtm.

Annual reports

Australian companies trading on the stock exchange are required to submit an annual report **every year** under the ASX listing rules. Shareholders receive a copy in the mail, although non-shareholders can also obtain a copy by contacting the listed company. Investment professionals recommend that investors refer to annual reports to review important information such as:

- a summary of a company's **operations** over the previous financial year
- **financial statements**, including balance sheets, from the past two years showing what the company owns and what it owes
- **profit and loss statements** revealing the company earnings during that financial year and explaining the distribution of those earnings
- **profit projections**
- information about **major shareholders** and company **directors**.

Annual reports and financial statements paint a picture of how well – or how badly – directors and management have been **running the company** over the past year. The figures and statements within are said to be useful tools for assessing the company's performance.

Company reports

More useful information can be found in the **balance sheets** (breakdown of company assets and liabilities), **income statements** (disclosure of expenses and profits or losses) and **cash flow statements** (tracking the movements of cash) of company reports.

The financial statements at the end of a company's report are said to be a good starting point for financial research. The **statement of financial position** shows what the company owns and what it owes. Investment professionals suggest that you look at the **balance sheet** and compare its **current assets** (what it owns) and **current liabilities** (what it owes), and compare the current year against the previous one.

Other useful company reports include **interim reports on the company's performance**, company **announcements** and **press releases** about new ventures or takeovers. Company reports should also contain details about the **directors**, the company's **dividend policy** and whether it pays **franked or unfranked dividends**.

STOCK ANALYSIS

The aim of stock analysis is to try to achieve an understanding of **past share price movements** and to form an opinion on their **future direction** to assist you in making an informed decision on whether to buy or sell. There are two main methods for predicting the performance of a company's share price:

- ◆ **Fundamental analysis** attempts to measure the 'intrinsic' value of a stock by looking at financial and economic data.
- ◆ **Technical analysis** looks at the trading history and stock price movement, usually using charts, in an attempt to identify patterns and trends.

Fundamental analysis

Fundamental analysis examines a company's **quantitative elements** to decide whether it provides a **good buying opportunity** – if the stock is underpriced – or a chance to sell because the stock is overpriced.

Quantitative analysis involves the valuation of companies using **mathematical tools**. Some of the most commonly used **quantitative factors** used in fundamental analysis are listed below.

Dividend yield

The dividend yield measures past performance and is the **actual return** on your investment in a company. This is calculated as:

$$\frac{\text{Dividend per share}}{\text{Market price of share}} \times \frac{100}{1}$$

This result will be a **percentage** of the current share price. If the dividend yield of a company is higher than the market average, it is said to represent a good buying opportunity.

Price to earnings ratio (P/E ratio)

The **P/E ratio** is a way of measuring market expectations of **company performance** and a means of comparing its shares against those in other companies to decide if they represent **good value**. It is calculated as:

$$\text{Current share price} \div \text{earnings per share}$$

A **high P/E ratio** indicates that the market has high expectations of strong profit growth, or it might indicate that the stock is **overpriced** and therefore a potential 'sell'. Theoretically, a **low P/E ratio** points towards a good 'buy' opportunity because it represents 'good value' meaning that you are paying less for a share than it is worth (i.e. its intrinsic value is greater).

The P/E ratio is said to be the most easily comprehended fundamental analysis tool and as a result it is widely used by the 'average' investor. Generally, market experts suggest that is a **useful starting point** for analysing whether or not to buy or sell a stock, but advise that it shouldn't be the only method used to weigh up a company's potential.

Earnings per share ratio (EPS) and return on equity (ROE)

Earnings per share is the amount of profit earned for every ordinary share issued, and is measured in **cents**.

Dividing these profits by the 'equity' – the assets of the company minus all the liabilities (this information can be found in company reports) – is known as **return on equity** or **ROE**. So:

$$\text{Return on equity (ROE)} = \frac{\text{Earnings per share}}{\text{Company assets} - \text{Liabilities}}$$

This measures **current performance** and is a major gauge of how well a company is performing. It is said to be a useful tool for comparing the profitability of various companies within a sector of the market and, on average, the higher the ROE, the better the investment.

A word about ratios

Share ratios can be used to relate a company's **financial information** to its **current share price**. They can act as a guide to how well the share price reflects a company's financial health and can be compared to other companies within the same industry (except for EPS which can't be applied for comparisons of different companies).

The EPS illustrates the **growth in earnings** from one year to the next, while the P/E ratio is possibly the most frequently applied gauge of **future earnings**.

This guide only provides a small sample of common fundamental analysis tools. There are many available and the Internet is a major source of information about them. The websites listed on page 18 are a good place to start.

Qualitative elements

The **qualitative aspects** are the **more subjective or less quantifiable elements** used to evaluate a company's future potential. These are many and varied – everything from the overall economy and industry conditions to the financial condition and management of companies. Some of the key factors to take into consideration are listed here.

Company management

While the results of fundamental analysis can provide valuable information to guide your investment decisions, if the management of a company is turning in a poor performance the share price is likely to suffer accordingly. Therefore, it's a good idea to carefully check out the **credentials and past performance** of the company directors and senior management to determine if they have consistently turned in superior performances. The **return on equity** calculation mentioned above can be useful for this.

When assessing the track record of management, market commentators note that the **CEO** and the **top four or five executives** generally exert the greatest influence on company performance – much more than the Board of Directors, as the hands-on managers are in charge of the day-to-day running of the organisation.

Company reports are a good source of information about the people in charge, their experience and their thoughts on the company's future performance. Be aware, however, that directors tend to focus on the corporate bright side. A search of the **ASIC website** at www.asic.gov.au can reveal if a company has breached ASIC guidelines – but not tell you if it has performed poorly.

Market outlook

Some basic **questions** to ask before taking the plunge into the market are:

- How fast is the company **growing**?
- Is the company **profitable** and likely to stay that way?
- Is this type of **business** currently doing well?
- Is the industry **shrinking or growing**?

Investment advisors recommend looking for companies with a **competitive edge** that can be maintained in the long term. Is the company forging ahead, lagging behind or keeping up with the pace of its competitors? They also emphasise the importance of examining the management's **track record**, the **performance and composition of the industry** in which it operates and the company's strategy for **growth and development**.

The company's documented **strategy or goals** – and whether it is positioned to achieve them – have been identified as key issues. Are there any new products or services on the drawing board, are existing ones being upgraded, are poorly performing parts of the business being dumped or are they moving into new markets and expanding their client base?

It's also important to be **aware** of:

- ◆ the **goods and services** that a company provides/produces.
- ◆ the **strength of demand** for its goods or services
- ◆ the relative strengths and weaknesses of its **competitors**.

Understanding the relationship between **supply** and **demand** for the company's products is a useful way to help determine its future prospects. Keep in mind that the stock exchange is a **marketplace** and, like all marketplaces, the prices of shares are influenced by supply and demand.

Future direction

In order to obtain a competitive edge in the market, companies must find new opportunities for **growth and profitability**. It's important to evaluate the factors that are likely to affect future performance and how the company plans to address them.

The changing **opinion** within the market about a company's prospects for future earnings can have a significant effect on the value of its shares. Major **company announcements** with profit implications tend to have a big impact on future share price direction. For example, if a mining company discovers a substantial new gold seam or a biotechnology company formulates a cure for cancer, the market will generally respond positively to the news. These types of events represent a major shot in the arm in relation to future company profits, leading to the likelihood of increasing demand for the stock and higher share values. Likewise, news of mergers, acquisitions and takeovers will also affect the direction of share prices.

Financial position

In order to assess a company's prospects, it's really important to examine its **financial position**. **Company reports** and **annual reports** are important sources of information of the company's operations over the past year. According to law, their contents should be deliver a **'true and fair' reflection** of business prospects. By reading the annual reports of companies, you can check out their activities over the past few years and establish how close they have come to achieving their forecasts.

Financial commentators suggest that investors take a close look at a company's profit forecast in the previous year's annual report. Then examine the **actual profits** achieved and **how they were achieved** against the forecast figures in order to evaluate the company's financial performance. Remember that sources of company profits are important, as some are more sustainable than others.

Other share market 'drivers'

Here are some factors that influence the **movements of the market**.

Economic events

The market reacts to new pieces of **economic information**. This may spark a big **'sell-off' or 'buy-up'** in certain sectors, depending on how the information is interpreted. This situation can lead to **dramatic price movements**. Government announcements affecting the economy can have a significant affect on share prices. These announcements include:

- **interest rate** movements
- balance of trade, employment, inflation, gross domestic product (GDP) or building **figures**
- imposition or lifting of **trade embargos**
- **elections** or changes to market-relevant **government policy**
- **wars** or **political conflicts** with market implications.

Interest rates

Interest rates play a central role in relation to the strength or weakness of the stock market and are a significant factor in determining its future direction. Interest rate movements in either direction are likely to have an impact on **prices**. Market experts point out that when interest rates **fall** there is good reason to believe that the market will move forward, while a **rise** in interest rates tends to provide the basis for share prices to drop. The market generally **anticipates** and moves ahead of changes in official interest rates by the Reserve Bank of Australia (RBA).

Company announcements

Certain **announcements** made by particular companies can affect share prices. The listing rules of the ASX demand that companies fulfil their obligation to keep the market **informed** of any developments that might affect the share price. As a result, they have to make constant reports to the ASX. These reports are broadcast 'live' to brokers' offices, as they may be price-sensitive, which means that market participants will act quickly on the information.

For example, trading in a stock will be **temporarily suspended** prior to any **price-sensitive announcements** such as major economic data, company profits or losses, mergers, takeovers or changes to the Board of Directors. This gives traders and investors the opportunity to amend or cancel orders.

The rumour mill

It's often commented that markets are **emotional**. A well-worn adage is that share prices are driven by **fear** and **greed**. As shares are bought and sold by mere mortals, it's inevitable that an element of psychology will creep in. Therefore, human behaviour and the fact that information – and its interpretation – plays such an important role in the direction of stock prices means that the rumour mill can be a powerful market-moving force.

Given that the market is said to look forward when price-sensitive information is due to be released by companies or governments, the market can make mountains out of molehills in **anticipation** of the news. **Rumours** of takeovers, business restructuring or speculation about future earnings forecasts can lead to the mass **dumping of stock** in a company which pushes prices down, or a **buying frenzy** which sends prices soaring.

Technical analysis

Technical analysis focuses on the **'technical' elements** of market activity. It explores **price and volume statistics** by studying a chart of historical price activity to predict **trends and outcomes** for share prices and how they will behave until the trend is interrupted. In contrast to fundamental analysis, charts focus on **investor psychology** and proponents say that they provide an accurate indication of **how the market behaves**. Critics of technical analysis are wary of the capability of charts to forecast market movements, preferring the analytical methods described above.

Technical analysts rely heavily on charts in an attempt to predict market patterns and identify trading opportunities. Their main analysis tools are indicators such as **support and resistance**, **moving averages** and **momentum**.

Some common **price modelling theories** are listed below. These are just a few examples and there are many more. A range of technical analysis tools can be found on **specialised websites**. Most **on-line stockbrokers** also offer these tools to their clients.

Moving averages

Moving averages show the **average value** of a share's price over a period of time. By adding up the closing prices from the past 50 days and dividing them by 50 you can determine the **50-day moving average**. The moving average will move because prices are constantly changing.

The most common moving averages are the 20, 30, 50, 100 and 200-day. The longer the timeframe, the less sensitive the moving average will be to price changes. Moving averages are used to stress the **path of a trend** and to level out **price and volume swings**.

Exponential Moving Average (EMA)

Exponential moving averages are calculated by applying a percentage of today's closing price to yesterday's moving average value. These calculations place more weight on **recent prices**.

Chaikin Money Flow Oscillator

Developed by Marc Chaikin, the **Chaikin Money Flow Oscillator** is calculated by subtracting a 10-day exponential moving average (EMA) from a three-day EMA. It works on the premise of tracking **buying pressure** (when a stock closes in the upper half of a period's trading range) and **selling pressure** (when a stock closes in the lower half of the period's trading range).

Relative Strength Index (RSI)

RSI is an indicator that **compares** the days that a stock finishes up **higher** against when it finishes **lower**. The RSI ranges from 0 to 100, but a stock is considered overbought if it reaches **70**, which means you should consider **selling**. Likewise, if the RSI approaches **30** it is a strong **buying indicator**. The RSI should be used as a complement to your other stock-picking tools, and not as a decision-maker.

Economy-related vs share-specific investing

Market commentators have identified two broad camps of investors: those whose share-trading decisions are based on **stock-specific** factors, or those who rely on **economy-related factors** (although some may have a foot in both camps).

According to this point of view, the majority of investors tend to focus more on the **share-specific factors** – financial data and conventional analysis tools like P/E ratios and dividend yields – to guide their investment decisions. These **'value investors'** tend to focus on the **future earnings** potential of a company. Value investing is the brainchild of the late Benjamin Graham who wrote *The Intelligent Investor* (HarperCollins, 1985), the investment 'bible' for fundamental analysts.

The other investment camp looks towards **economy-related factors**. These investors make their decisions based on the **bigger economic picture**, broad market movements and the price cycle of shares in specific companies. In other words, they buy and sell shares according to the economic outlook and stock market trends.

Conversely, value investors typically disregard market trends. They believe that buying a share at a discount to its intrinsic value – using fundamental analysis to look at share-specific factors – is the key to successful investing. While the experts are divided on which is best, both approaches have strong supporters. However, neither is touted as being foolproof.

Warning signs

The main reason to spend time and effort on thoroughly researching and analysing companies is to determine their **health and prospects**. While this is an essential a part of the share trading process – and can make the difference between returning a profit or making a loss – it is not fail-safe. There are, however, some **common warning signs** when a company isn't performing well.

- If a company issues a **profit warning** or **downgrade**, a fall in its stock price tends to follow. If it suffers a **huge loss** it may take some time before they recover in value.

- Another thing to watch out for is the market holding a strong **negative opinion** about a company or industry. This of particular concern if a company's competitors are putting in a much better performance.

- The payment of dividends is linked to a company's profitability. Therefore, you might find that a company isn't paying its shareholders a **dividend** due to an **unexpected loss** over the quarterly reporting season or the financial year. Keep in mind, however, that this isn't always a warning sign. The media giant NewsCorp is one of the most liquid companies in the market but it tends not to pay dividends because profits are channelled back into building the business.

- **Share buy-backs** can occur when the people in charge of running a company believe that investors and the market undervalue its shares. As a result, the company may attempt to **buy back some stock** from its shareholders. Smaller shareholdings or **unmarketable parcels** may be targeted during a share buy-back and sometimes brokerage fees are absorbed by the company.

- On occasion, a sudden and **significant fall in the value of the company** can be an ominous sign. There could be a large scale dumping of the stock and the share price may drop dramatically. This happened during the **'tech wreck' in 2000**, when investors were no longer keen to hold shares in particular companies or the technology sector itself. Companies can also become the target of **takeovers**, **mergers** or **acquisitions** if the value of their stock falls dramatically.

- Interestingly, market commentators have noted that often it's the company being taken over that experiences a sudden increase in share price, while the company at the helm of the acquisition suffers a corresponding fall in its share price while the market digests the news. However, one important thing to remember is that the value of stocks in **'quality' companies** will tend to **recover** eventually. A sharp fall in share value is by no means always a fatal prognosis.

MAKING YOUR MOVE INTO THE MARKET

There are **three basic investment strategies** to consider when building a share portfolio. Which one you choose will be driven by your investment goals, risk profile, income, age and investment time horizon.

- If you are focused on securing an **income stream**, perhaps to meet your living expenses, **income shares** that tend to pay **franked dividends** may be your chosen strategy.
- If a secure income stream isn't your overriding concern, you might decide that **growth stocks** are the way to go. Capital growth can help you to **accumulate wealth** and provides a hedge against inflation. On the flipside, shares offering capital growth can also result in **capital losses** – and the shares with the greatest growth potential may also carry the greatest risk of loss.
- Finally, you might opt for a **mix of income and growth shares**. In this way you can enjoy the benefits of a **secure income stream**, whilst achieving some measure of **capital growth**.

The best way to minimise your risks and maximise your potential investment returns is to invest in **quality shares** regularly and to hold onto them for at least **seven to ten years** to ride out the market's inevitable peaks and troughs.

What is a 'quality' share?

While a lot of variables come into play, the basic rule of thumb is to buy **stocks in quality companies**. Large, established companies like Woolworths, Coca Cola, BHP Billiton and TAB tend to fall under the umbrella of **income stocks**. Typically, income stocks operate in **highly regulated industries** and are usually **defensive** in nature, being among the least volatile of all stocks. Even when the share value isn't racing ahead in leaps and bounds, you will usually receive a twice-yearly dividend.

A number of **growth stocks** would also be considered as 'quality' investments or blue chips. These include the big banks – Commonwealth, ANZ, Westpac and NAB – and some of the media, telecommunications and health care/biotechnology powerhouses like NewsCorp, Telstra and Cochlear. These are large companies that have become household names, operating in more **dynamic industries**. One of the hallmarks of a quality growth stock is said to be the maintaining of consistently **faster-than-average growth**. They continually seek **new opportunities** to build their businesses.

Market experts warn that even shares in quality companies, including the 'blue chips', may record a **poor performance** and fall in value at various times. However, as share prices do bounce back in the long term, the consensus is that you shouldn't be afraid to buy quality stocks just because others are selling them, since you may be buying into a quality at a rock-bottom price. Also, commentators have noted that companies can fall victim to **'market fashion'** and can in fact be performing well in a business sense when the stock price is lagging behind.

Does size equal quality?

It's also widely recognised that shares in smaller or **less established companies** tend to be regarded as **'lower' quality** because they are usually more exposed to the vagaries of the shifting economy and competition from larger companies in the marketplace. For these reasons, amongst others, they carry a **higher risk** of not achieving their profit forecasts, and they can even collapse. In contrast, shares in larger **companies** with well-known brands, good business models, first-class management and diversified income streams are more likely to be thought of as **'quality' shares**. However, in line with the **'risk = reward'** axiom, smaller companies can be well-positioned to deliver higher returns. Their size and flexibility allows them to manoeuvre quickly to capitalise on gaps in the market and maintain their profitability more easily than larger corporations. As a result, the value of their shares can rise significantly.

A series of well-publicised, big-name **corporate collapses** in 2001, including HIH Insurance, OneTel and Ansett, has demonstrated that large and/or established companies **aren't immune to failure**. The writing didn't appear on the wall until it was too late for the shareholders – both large and small. The concept of 'quality' in relation to companies can therefore be difficult to pin down with complete certainty.

On the back of the highly publicised 2002 USA corporate accounting scandals, investment advisers and market commentators in Australia have widely been reported as saying that investors should look beyond **'accounting' profits** (found in company reports) and concentrate on the business's reported **cash profit** instead. Cash profits are said to be a better gauge of a company's performance because accounting-based figures have been shown to be unreliable as they don't always reveal the whole story about company earnings. However, it has been pointed out that due to Australia's strong **regulatory regime** and more **transparent corporate accounting** practices, scandals on the US scale are unlikely to erupt on our market.

The lesson learnt from these recent failures is that **size doesn't always equal quality**. Since these collapses, the spotlight has been turned more than ever on corporate accounting practices and the people who run the businesses. At this point it's worth taking on board the advice of Warren Buffet, hailed as the world's best-known and most successful investor. He advocates buying shares in **growing businesses** that have comparatively **predictable earnings** and a **sustainable competitive edge**, as these factors will contribute to **increasing company value** and a higher share price in the long term.

Diversification

The concept of **risk** has already been touched upon and for most investors the idea of 'risk' translates into concern about **losing a large chunk of their investment** outlay. Therefore, it's important to build a portfolio that is **spread across the market** to enable you to manage your risk, protect the value of your investment and increase the chance of profit. The best way to diversify is to buy shares from **a range of companies and industries**, **sectors** and even **countries**.

Holding shares in just **one or two companies** is very **risky**, and as a general rule of thumb, many investment advisors recommend that you invest in at least ten (ideally 15–20) different companies across a variety of **sectors**. A sector is comprised of **similar companies**. For example:

♦ the **Media sector** is home to companies like the Ten Network and News Corporation
♦ the **Transportation sector** contains Qantas and Brambles Industries
♦ BHP Billiton and Rio Tinto are in the **Materials** sector.

MAJOR MARKET SECTORS

Automobiles and Components	Insurance
Banks	Materials
Capital Goods	Media
Commercial Services and Supplies	Pharmaceuticals and Biotechnology
Consumer Durables and Apparel	Real Estate
Diversified Finances	Retailing
Energy	Software and Services
Food and Staples Retailing	Technology Hardware and Equipment
Food, Beverages and Tobacco	Telecommunication Services
Health Care Equipment and Services	Transportation
Hotels, Restaurants and Leisure	Utilities

Cycles

Market experts point out that the key to diversification is selecting stocks that don't share tendencies to **rise or fall in price** simultaneously. The economy goes through **cycles**, and business earnings (and share prices) within specific industries or sectors can be affected in very different ways.

The various market sectors **do not all move in unison** and at times, some will perform better than others. For instance, the Food and Household Goods sector and the Banking and Finance sector are home to disparate companies and operate in different parts of the economy. Therefore, they may not be similarly affected by a particular set of economic data. In times of economic uncertainty, for example, the market tends to favour defensive stocks such as gold. When consumer confidence is low, some retailers and tourism operators might suffer lower share values.

Balancing risk and reward

The best way to **balance risk and reward** is by not putting all your investment eggs into one basket.

If you build a **diversified portfolio of quality shares** across a number of sectors, in seven to ten years those companies are likely to record **continued growth** allowing you to reap the rewards of **increased share value**. However, a diversified portfolio involves the art of compromise. The protection provided by diversification means that your **overall investment return might be less** than that of an undiversified portfolio.

This is where the '**risk = reward**' axiom applies. Over the long term a diversified portfolio provides steadier – but possibly lower – returns by offering **some insurance** against market cycles. If you want to **minimise risk** you must be prepared to accept **lower returns**.

Types of risk

There are **three broad areas of risk** that investors should be aware of.

- ◆ **Investor risk** relates to our own actions rather than market forces. Inadequate diversification will increase this risk, as will selling shares at the wrong time (rather than holding on for the long term) and 'timing' your entry into the market by trying to pick highs and lows.
- ◆ **Portfolio risk** can be managed by adequately diversifying your portfolio – buying at least ten quality shares across a range of companies, sectors and even countries or other asset classes.
- ◆ **Share market risk** is beyond an investor's control and can't be minimised by portfolio diversification. However, history has consistently shown that the share market does bounce back after its downturns.

International vs local shares

Another way to diversify your portfolio is by adding **international shares**. You can become a 'global share owner' instead of pinning your investment strategy on a market that comprises less than 2% of the value of all the companies trading on world stock markets. As the Australian and international markets tend not to perform in unison, buying overseas shares can **lessen your total portfolio risk** by helping to even out some of the fluctuations in different markets.

International shares have historically earned **higher returns** than local shares. Between **1985 and 2001**, international shares outperformed domestic shares by returning **15.4% against 13.9%** (see table on page 8).

If you look at **individual years**, the varied fortunes of the two markets become much more apparent. For example:

- In **1997**, Australian shares returned a reasonable 12.2%, while international equities returned a massive 41.6%.
- In **2001** investors saw a shift in fortunes on the back of a global economic slowdown and the extraordinary political events following the September 11 terrorist attacks on the USA. As a result, share prices were sharply **driven down**.

Since then, the market has staged a recovery and Australian shares finished the year in **positive territory**, posting a return of just over 10% for 2001, whereas **international shares fell** by around 10%. Diversifying across a number of share markets around the world provides the opportunity to take advantage of the better performing markets, whilst lessening the impact of the poorer performing ones.

Pros and cons

You have the choice of investing in companies and industries in the major markets of North America, Western Europe and Japan or the emerging markets of Asia and Latin America. Generally speaking, **US and West European markets** tend to present **similar risks** to investing in shares **domestically**. On the other hand, investing in **emerging markets** carries the **highest level of risk** for economic and political reasons. To balance the risks, many market experts recommend a ratio of around 30% to 40% international to 60% or 70% Australian shares for a well-diversified share portfolio.

The main benefits of investing in international shares are **diversification** and access to around **98% of the world's share markets** with the potential to achieve superior long-term returns. However, overseas markets can be more **volatile**, with sharper rises and falls. **Overseas political events** can also affect share values and returns, as can fluctuations in Australian or world **currencies**, because gains or losses must be converted back to

Australian dollars. It's also important to note that you **cannot** receive **fully franked dividends** from international shares.

Accessing overseas markets

Finally, while it is possible to buy shares **directly in international companies**, the process can be more complicated and time-consuming than investing locally. Therefore, investing via an **international share fund** that selects the shares and manages your investment is advisable for the average investor. You can choose from global, regional, single country or emerging market funds.

The simplest way to invest in overseas markets is via a **managed fund**. Australian investors can access them through companies like AMP, AXA, Colonial First State, Bankers Trust (BT), Rothschild, MLC, Hunter Hall, Invesco, Dresdner, HSBC, Perpetual and Vanguard. Contact a **financial adviser** for more information, or speak with the fund managers.

Time in the market vs market timing

It has become an investment cliché but it rings very true:

> Time in the market is more important than
> trying to time market entry and exit.

'**Buying low and selling high**' is the ultimate goal of share market investors. However, trying to figure out when is the best time to buy or sell is an inexact science and it can be nerve-wracking and costly. **Market timing is a dangerous game**, more the domain of 'day traders' than 'investors'. It is incredibly risky. Market commentators point out that you may lose money if you sell too soon and the market rises shortly afterwards, or if you sell too late, based on your perception that the market has peaked when it is in fact starting to fall.

It is a rare, almost mythical, investor who can consistently **predict** with any level of precision when – and by how much – share prices will go up or down. As mentioned earlier, the market is driven by **greed and fear**. More often than not, a lot of people tend to buy shares when the market is at a high and when everyone else is also buying. Likewise, when there is a downturn in the market people tend to start dumping their shares, often at a loss. Most investment advisors say that the average investor would be more likely to benefit by regularly buying shares **over a period of time**, rather than trying to make a **quick killing**. However, the biggest risk is often said to be **not investing at all** due to a fear of losing your money.

Dollar cost averaging

Because market timing is fraught with pitfalls, the safest strategy is **dollar cost averaging**.

This is a relatively simple strategy that eliminates the risk associated with timing entry into the share market by **investing regularly** with a **fixed amount of money** each pay period, weekly or monthly, to top up your share portfolio. By following this strategy, you are able to buy more shares when the market is down (and prices are low) and less when the market is up (and prices are high). It works by **averaging out the cost of the shares** you buy over an extended period, even though the underlying share prices are constantly rising and falling.

Dollar cost averaging is an **affordable** way of building your share portfolio and a good way to ride out the market's highs and lows. Even though you might miss out on a **bargain buy** at some stage, you'll also insulate yourself against buying when a share's price soars. It can also save you some sleepless nights by **avoiding the stress and uncertainty** of trying to time your buying decisions.

Key things to remember

- ◆ **The length time in the market** is an key issue in relation to higher risk assets like shares – the longer you hold onto them, the greater your potential for **maximum investment returns**.
- ◆ If you hold onto a **diversified portfolio of shares** for **seven to ten years** they are likely to increase in value and bounce back from any short-term losses (the market moves up and down on a yearly, monthly, weekly and daily basis, and can move by as much as 5% on a single day).
- ◆ Set your **financial goals**, mobilise an **appropriate investment strategy** and then stick to it.
- ◆ Keep in mind the **investment goals and timeframes** that you set when mobilising your plan to buy shares.
- ◆ Be **flexible:** you might want to take a profit or sell off part of your portfolio if your personal or financial circumstances change.
- ◆ **Jumping in and out of the market** could eat away at your share portfolio. Sit tight and see out your investment strategy to its conclusion wherever possible.
- ◆ **Remember your time horizon.** If you set out to invest for eight years in order to realise a certain level of return, try to ride out the plan to achieve your long-term financial goals.

SHARE FLOATS

'Listing' on the ASX

As well as trading on the market, another way of buying shares is via a **'float'**. When a company decides to **'list' on the Australian Stock Exchange (ASX)** it is required to lodge a **prospectus** with the Australian Securities and Investments Commission (ASIC) and all potential investors must be issued with a copy. Usually a company lists on the ASX because it needs **funds** in order to build the business, so shares are offered to the public via an **initial public offering (IPO)**, or 'float', to **raise capital**.

Why do companies 'float'?

In recent years, there have been a number of **major IPOs**, including Telstra, TAB and the Commonwealth Bank, as well as numerous lower-profile floats. As a result, the number of Australians who are shareholders has **increased significantly** – per capita, we have one the highest rates of share ownership in the world. As well as the incentive of securing shares at a potentially lower price, another financial benefit of buying shares through floats is the **saving on brokerage fees**.

While shares offered in an IPO can shoot up in value when they start trading on the ASX, not all floats are a resounding success. Sometimes shares will **fall in value** when they start trading on the market, so you shouldn't assume that IPOs are guaranteed to make you money. It's really important that you go over the prospectus with a fine-tooth comb and understand the details of the share issue, the company, what it does, what it's planning to do in the future and its likelihood of being profitable.

The prospectus

There is some concern in the investment community that the public treat a prospectus as the superfluous 'wrapper' around the float application form, rather than vital information for evaluating the prospects of the company. It actually serves a dual purpose in **striving to inform** and **trying to entice**. Snappy marketing copy tries to persuade you to jump onboard, while factual information provides important details to help you gauge the viability of the investment. According to ASIC, under the *Corporations Act* prospectuses must contain all relevant information to allow you to make an **informed evaluation of the company's prospects** by disclosing full details of the company and share issue. These include:

- the **cost** of the shares in the IPO
- **minimum** and **maximum** share amounts

- **information** about the **directors** and **senior management**
- **directors' reports**
- a **full run-down** of the type of business, its products and services
- **financial reports** (historical data and profit reports and projections)
- the **assumptions** on which profit forecasts are based
- the **purpose** of the share issue
- how the **capital** will be used
- **potential risks** associated with the listing.

The ASIC website is an excellent source of comprehensive information about floats and prospectuses and is definitely worth a visit to get a better understanding of IPOs. You can also search the ASIC offer list database at www.fido.asic.gov.au for upcoming floats or call the ASIC Infoline on 1300 300 630 to find out if a prospectus has been lodged.

Applying for shares

You can obtain a prospectus **directly from the listing company** or through the participating **broker/s**. Most brokers provide information about the IPOs in which they are involved on their own **websites**. The ASX also provides information on upcoming floats (www.asx.com.au) as does ASIC (www.asic.gov.au) and the Float Tank website (www.floattank.com.au).

The only way to apply for shares in an IPO is by **completing and signing the form** attached to the prospectus. A cheque for the amount of shares you intend to buy must be attached and sent to the broker **underwriting** (organising) the float, or to the relevant **Share Registry**. The new shares are offered to the public at a predetermined price and after the company has listed the shares they can only be traded on the ASX via a **broker**.

It's worth noting that while most listing companies may choose to allocate a portion of the shares to the general public, there are instances where some people receive **preferential treatment**. For example, NRMA members were lucky enough to receive free shares in NRMA, while other interested investors had to wait until the shares commenced trading on the ASX. Likewise, with some smaller or highly select floats, shares are not available to all comers – they may only be open to clients of **full-service brokers** who are underwriting the float or have a firm broker allocation. Occasionally discount brokers also participate in IPOs and they are allocated a portion of the shares to distribute amongst their clients.

Minimum share allocations

Frequently floats will specify a **minimum allocation of shares** which is **the lowest amount of shares** that each investor will receive. This tends to make floats more equitable, as all applicants are more likely to receive a minimum allocation. However, obtaining shares through an IPO can sometimes be a case of **'get in early or miss the boat'**. If it is **oversubscribed** – meaning there are insufficient shares to meet investor demand – the sooner you return your application to your broker or the Share Registry, the better your chances of receiving an allocation.

In some cases, the minimum subscription may be **reduced even further**. For example, the demand for TAB shares was so strong that the final minimum allocation for retail investors was only 243 shares.

It's important to note that the directors of a company are **not legally required to fill your request** for shares in a float. As long as the shares are issued according to the terms and conditions specified in the prospectus they are not required to allocate shares to all float subscribers. Therefore, if a listing is oversubscribed you may not receive an allocation and your cheque will be returned.

Investment reality check

- ✓ Don't think you have all the answers and don't be afraid to **ask questions** – overconfidence or uneducated guesses can be the kiss of death for a share portfolio.
- ✓ Adequately **diversify** your share portfolio – don't put all your investment eggs in one basket.
- ✓ Don't buy shares based on '**hot tips**' or second-hand speculation.
- ✓ Don't count on shares to **continue their winning streak** forever. 'Form' can change from year to year – the shares may no longer be in the race.
- ✓ Do your **research** – or pay a qualified professional to give you advice.
- ✓ Don't invest purely for **tax reasons**. Look at the quality of the shares in which you're investing. The key is underlying viability, rather than just reducing tax liability.
- ✓ Invest for the **long term** (seven to ten years). Don't fritter away your investment capital on a doomed quest to pick the highs and lows by quickly diving in and out of stocks.
- ✓ Don't try to **time** buying and selling decisions – even professional traders and experienced analysts can't do it with total precision. Reduce your risk by **dollar cost averaging** instead.
- ✓ Set your **investment goals** and time horizons – and sit tight. Don't expect immediate gratification from the share market.
- ✓ Don't **panic sell** – shares in quality companies will bounce back in the long term.

KEEPING TRACK OF YOUR SHARES

Monitoring the performance of your share portfolio is an important part of managing your investment strategy. Even though you should hold shares for seven to ten years it isn't a good idea to file them away and not revisit them until this time has passed. Market experts recommend that you review blue chip portfolios **at least every three months** and certainly no less than once a year. You may need to weed out some losers and top up on shares that are likely to put in a better performance. The market is unpredictable and if you don't keep track of your portfolio it's almost impossible to tell if your investment strategy is going according to plan.

Monitoring your shares can be reasonably straightforward. Amongst the things to look out for are **share price movements**, **profit forecasts** issued by the companies and any factors affecting the **future earnings** and **profitability** of the companies in which you are a shareholder. (These are the same factors you should have looked for when you first invested.)

Where to find information

A good way to track your shares is via the **Internet**. There are a huge number of sites (see table on page 18) that provide easy access to **share market prices** including the current **'bid'**, **'offer'**, **volumes** and **'last sale'** that give a a an indication of the current performance of your shares at a glance. However, some sites are delayed by 20 minutes. If you are an on-line broker client or website subscriber you can log in and get a **'live' snapshot of the market** with real-time prices. You can also access more detailed information like **'market depth'**, showing how many buyers and sellers are queued up at a particular price at different price 'steps'.

Share tables

The **share tables** published in the finance section of the daily national newspapers and *The Australian Financial Review* also help you to **track your shares** on a daily basis. They provide basic information such as:

- the highest and lowest **sale price** of the day
- the **52-week high and low**
- the total **volume of stock** (in hundreds) traded on the previous day
- the **last sale**
- the **annualised dividend** ('Div c per share')
- **P/E ratios**
- **dividend yields**.

Shares prices are usually listed **alphabetically** by company name according to the **ASX code**. For example, Coles Myer is abbreviated to 'CML' and Westpac is 'WBC'. The layout and level of detail in share tables can vary from publication to publication. Some magazines, such as *Shares*, offer **more detailed information** and more tables including bonus share plans, dividend reinvestment plans, preference shares, dividends declared and company reports.

Share tables glossary

52-week high and low	The highest and lowest price at which an ASX listed share has traded in that year. Enables you to check the current share price against the 52-week high and low.
ASX code or company	The ASX code is an abbreviation of a company name. Codes can be searched on the ASX website at www.asx.com.au or on-line broker websites.
+ or −	The change in share price (in cents) from the previous 'close' of trading.
Vol. or no. sold (100s)	The total volume of shares (in 100s) traded over the course of the previous trading day. It serves as an indicator of market interest in a stock (both positive and negative).
Trading day high and low	The price range over which a share traded on the most recent ASX trading day. A measure of volatility (rises and falls in the stock). Useful as a short-term snapshot of performance.
Last sale	The last price at which the shares were traded on the ASX. Useful for checking your shareholding's current value at a glance.
Closing quotes – buy (bid) and offer (sell)	The highest price someone is prepared to pay and the lowest price at which someone is willing to sell a particular stock. Unlike the **'last sale'**, shares are not always traded at these prices.
Dividend c per share	Up-to-date annualised dividend paid by the company per share. An **'f'** means fully franked dividend and **'p'** means a partly franked dividend.
Div. yield %	The actual return on an investment, calculated daily, by dividing the dividend rate by the current share price and expressing it as a percentage. It only measures past performance.
Earn share c	The profit earned per ordinary share.
P/E ratio	The current market price of a share divided by its estimated future earnings per share and one of the most frequently used indicators of future earnings. It is said to be a useful guide for showing how much the market is willing to pay for a stock.

CHOOSING A STOCKBROKER

There are numerous **stockbrokers** to meet the various requirements of all investors, offering different levels of **trading products and services**. The choice of stockbroker is an important one, since it is stockbrokers who facilitate the **buying and selling** of shares on the ASX. They are your **link to the market** and play an important role in the execution of your investment strategy.

Finding a stockbroker who best suits you is an important part of the investing process and involves the making of several **decisions** based on:

- your level of investment **knowledge**
- **market confidence**
- the **time** you have available to **research** shares
- access to **technology** (eg. the Internet)
- range of **services and products** required
- **costs**.

So, how do you decide what type of broker is the right one for you?

There are **three main categories** of stockbroker available to Australian investors:

- **full service** brokers, who offer advice
- **discount** brokers, who simply execute your orders
- **on-line** brokers, who provide the facilities for conducting share transactions via the Internet.

Some brokers (such as Goldman Sachs JB Were and Macquarie Financial Services) are now covering **all three bases**.

The **cost** of brokerage varies depending on the level of service offered. The one thing that brokers should all have in common is an **Australian Financial Services Licence**. All stockbrokers trading on the ASX must be licensed by the Australian and Securities and Investment Commission (ASIC).

Full service brokers

In the past, full service brokers dominated the stockbroking landscape and they continue to satisfy the demand from investors looking for expert guidance. They employ teams of investment professionals (equity analysts) who **analyse** and continually review ASX listed companies and **provide recommendations** on which shares to buy, sell and hold. They also employ private client advisors who interact with clients to build and manage share portfolios based on the investors' requirements. But this level of research and personal advice comes at a cost – these brokers charge **higher brokerage fees**.

A full service broker usually charges between 1% and 2.5% per share transaction, depending on the size of the transaction, with a **minimum fee** starting at **$75 to $100**. Often, the bigger the size of the transaction, the lower the percentages of brokerage charged, and in some cases fees are negotiable. In effect, you are paying full service brokers to **construct and manage** your investment portfolio.

Often, investors will use full service brokers if they are **uncertain** about selecting their own stocks or if they don't have the **time or expertise** to manage their portfolio. Some full service brokers tend to focus on high net-worth clients who have **substantial shareholdings**. Others, however, are happy to take on smaller clients.

Examples of **full service brokers** include:

- Goldman Sachs JB Were
- Burrell Stockbroking
- Salomon Smith Barney
- Macquarie Financial Services
- ABN Amro Morgans
- UBS Warburg (Private)

CHECKLIST: FULL SERVICE BROKERS

- ✓ **Do your research**. Contact several firms to make sure that you feel comfortable with their investment style and that they understand your investment needs.
- ✓ **Find out how much contact** you can expect to have with your private client advisor to decide if the level of interaction suits you.
- ✓ Ask how actively and frequently they **review share portfolios**.
- ✓ Check the **cost of brokerage** per trade.
- ✓ Investigate the depth and scope of the broker's **research facilities** to make sure that you are getting the best possible advice.
- ✓ Ask if they provide advice on and access to **other products** like high-demand floats, international shares, bonds, listed trusts, equity trusts, a range of managed funds and cash management accounts.

Discount brokers

Discount brokers have carved out a niche the market in recent years and have captured their fair share of Australian investors. Many have chosen to go it alone by opting for **lower brokerage rates** over advice and higher fees. Their brokerage rates are cheaper because they only execute your trades and do not offer advice. Brokerage rates are competitive and range from around **$33 to around $66** per trade – and approximately 1% of trade value for large

trades. Discount brokers offer **over-the-phone** trading facilities where you can place your order with a broker representative. Most also offer access to **on-line trading**. Some examples of **discount brokers** are:

- Sanford Securities
- Rivkin Discount Stockbroking
- Merrill Lynch HSBC
- WealthPoint Financial Services

Investors who are confident about **selecting their own stocks** tend to use discount stockbrokers. If you are not, it might be advisable to go with a full service broker.

CHECKLIST: DISCOUNT BROKERS

✓ Compare the brokerage **costs** of different brokers.
✓ Check out their range of services to see if they offer:
- **Internet trading**
- fast access to brokers representatives when placing **over-the-phone orders** – waiting in a telephone queue can be frustrating and costly if the market is moving quickly
- a 1300 or toll-free phone number for regional and inter-state clients
- access to **other financial products** and **services**
- free **newsletters**
- free **on-line company research and analysis tools**
- **discounted brokerage rates** for frequent traders

On-line brokers

On-line brokers are the most recent entrants into the broking arena. They rode into town on the technology wave that has given investors even more choice over how they buy and sell shares – as well as the lowest brokerage rates.

On-line brokers offer the **cheapest brokerage rates** – starting at about **$9.99** for up to $10 000 trade value. Once in place, technology is more cost-effective than over-the-phone service involving humans. However, **fees can vary** from broker to broker – up to $66 per trade – depending on the level of technology, research and value-added services on offer. Like discount brokers, most of these brokers **do not offer advice** so investors must be **confident selecting stocks**.

The **timing** is very important when placing a buy or sell order as the market can move away from your target price quickly and delays can be costly. Many on-line brokers offer **'straight through processing'**, which means that your order is sent directly to the Stock Exchange Automated

Trading System (SEATS). With some brokers, when orders are received via the broker's website they are then entered into SEATS **manually** by an operator – much like the process involved in placing an over-the-phone order. Therefore, access to the market is not instantaneous.

It's important to be aware that with on-line brokers you are very much 'flying solo' in terms of correctly placing, amending and cancelling orders. If you are trading via a straight through processing broker you do not have the safety net of someone on the other end double-checking your orders. Trading technology tends to be quite sophisticated, though, and often really obvious errors, like mistakenly entering the quantity in the price field, is picked up by a checking mechanism. However, the onus is on you to ensure that **all the details** of the order (eg. price, quantity and stock codes) are **correct**. Trading errors can be expensive.

Examples of **larger on-line brokers** are CommSec, E*TRADE, National and Westpac.

CHECKLIST: ON-LINE BROKERS

✓ Does the broker offer access to **straight through order processing**?

✓ Is there fast and reliable access to **electronic order confirmation** to avoid doubling up on an order – potentially a very expensive mistake? You need to know that your order has been received, entered onto the market and fully or partially executed or cancelled.

✓ Does the broker offer prompt access to humans for order placement or confirmation if the technology fails?

✓ Does the broker offer **free access to services** like company research, analysis tools, company news, ASX announcements and price alerts?

✓ Do they offer multiple **watch lists, real time data** and a good level of **market depth**?

Finding a broker

Once you have decided which type of broker is right for you, the next step is relatively simple. Your first port of call in the search for a broker could be the **ASX broker referral service** which provides a list of full service, discount and on-line brokers. Go to www.asx.com.au or phone 1300 300 279.

Other options include:

◆ word of mouth: ask friends, family or work colleagues who have used a broker for their first-hand **recommendations**

- check the listings in the **Yellow Pages** directory
- surf the **Internet** (see the list of useful websites on page 18 for a starting point).

Most importantly, **do your homework**. Shop around for the best deal based on your trading requirements, the level of service and cost.

Disputes

As a rule, stockbrokers are highly qualified and experienced professionals. It is in their interest to act in the **best interests** of their clients, and most of the time you'll find that this is the case. Before you open a trading account with a full service broker, ask for a copy of their **Financial Services Guide**. As well as verifying that the broking firm is **licensed** with ASIC, it provides information about how they deal with **trading disputes** and other **complaints** relating to advice and service. Given the nature of the trading process, occasionally **trading disputes** will arise between a client and a broker. For this reason, all trading-related phone calls are recorded to verify 'who said what' and help in settling disputes – discount brokers also tape calls. Therefore, your first course of action would be to contact your broker to resolve the issue directly.

Unfortunately, in some cases there is an impasse and this is where the services of the **Financial Industry Complaints Service (FICS)** can be useful. This organisation provides **free advice and assistance** to consumers of financial products, including shares sold by licensed security dealers (stockbrokers).

As part of their licensing agreements, all **investment advisors** dealing with retail clients are required to be **members of FICS**. When an investor's complaint amounts to less than $100 000, FICS is a far better option than suing your broker. Members are bound by any FICS decision, but the complainant retains the **right to sue** if they are not satisfied with the decision.

Another course of action – if talks with your broker fail to satisfactorily resolve the trading dispute – is to register your complaint with ASIC on 1300 300 630. See their website at www.fido.asic.gov.au for more information.

GETTING STARTED

Before you can buy or sell shares, you will have to do some paperwork and open a **trading account** with your chosen broker. You will be required to complete and sign **documentation** disclosing details such as your name, address, occupation, tax file number (TFN), Australian resident status and you might even have to provide identification. By law, **minors** (under the age of 18) are **not permitted** to open share-trading accounts in their own right. However, a parent or guardian can open a trading account in 'trust' on the budding young investor's behalf.

You might also have to set up a specific **cash management account (CMA)** via your broker for the settlement of trades, with an initial minimum deposit usually starting at **$1000**. Brokers tend to use a specific CMA that will be linked to your trading account. You can't nominate your regular bank account, as brokers are unable to access your funds in these types of accounts. The **cost of the shares** bought through that broker and the **brokerage fee** will be automatically pulled from this account. Also, any profits from the sale of shares will be paid straight into your CMA. Some brokers will let you settle trades by cheque – although on-line brokers usually insist on a CMA.

Share 'sponsorship'

Before you start trading you must also decide about the **sponsorship of your shares**. This is mandatory, and there are two options.

1 Broker sponsored shares

The first option is to become **broker sponsored**. You must complete and sign a **CHESS sponsorship form** provided by your broker of choice and you will then be issued with a **Holder Identification Number (HIN)** for all your nominated shareholdings. Being 'broker sponsored' simplifies the share selling process because your holding can be **instantly confirmed** and the order can then be placed onto the market. You can choose to be sponsored by **more than one broker**, however, if want to sell shares sponsored by one broker through another broker you must first conduct a **transfer** by providing the selling broker with a **CHESS transfer form**. **CHESS transfers take time** to process, so you will not be able to sell your shares until the transfer is complete.

2 Issuer sponsored shares

The other choice is **issuer sponsorship** where proof of your share ownership is registered with a **Share Registry**. You will be allocated a **Shareholder**

Registration Number (SRN), which identifies and registers your shareholding in a particular company. If you choose issuer sponsorship, a separate SRN will be issued for **each one of your shareholdings**. Unlike the HIN, which covers all shares sponsored by a broker, you could end up with multiple SRNs. You also need to be aware that SRNs and the details of your shareholdings aren't transparent in the broker's system as is the case with HINs, therefore, when you place a sell order the onus is on you to confirm **how many shares you own**.

Share settlement

The introduction of **CHESS** – the **Clearing House Electronic Subregister System** – in 1994 marked the decline of the manual, paper-based 'scrip' system in favour of the efficiencies of technology. CHESS has eliminated the need for companies to issue **share certificates** to their shareholders. And shareholders have, in turn, been freed from the responsibility of safeguarding their share certificates to make sure they do not go missing in action! This information is now securely stored in the **ASX database** and shareholdings are registered electronically with the company/companies in which you've bought shares or with your stockbroker. The introduction of CHESS has also sped up the **settlement process** – when shares are bought or sold they are electronically transferred from broker to broker.

In Australia there is a **three-day settlement period** for share transactions following the purchase or sale of shares. It's known as the **T+3 system** (the day of trade + three business days). This means that shares must be paid for, cleared and delivered within this timeframe.

Your first trade

Before you place an order, it's important to note that the ASX has set the minimum value of buy orders at $500 – no restrictions apply to sell orders, so they can be of lower value. Another condition imposed on first-time investors in a particular company is that the initial share purchase must be in the form of a **marketable parcel**. The number of shares in marketable parcel can vary from stock to stock and is determined by the company's share price. This 'rule' for buy orders does not tend to apply to the subsequent trades in that stock.

To add to the list of conditions for first-time share investors, brokers generally impose their own **minimum values** for share purchases in a particular stock. As a guide, they usually range from **$1000 to $3000**, although they can vary from broker to broker. Also, most brokers insist that you have **sufficient funds** to cover the cost of your first buy order – usually lodged by cheque or deposit into a cash management account prior to placing the trade.

Alternatively, you can use **collateral** in the form of **other shareholdings** that are sponsored by the broker with whom you place the order.

How does the ASX trading system work?

When a lot of people think of the stock market, the image that still springs to mind is a hectic trading floor crammed with wildly gesticulating, phone-wielding brokers' reps barking orders at unflappable chalkies on the high boards. While this scene is based on reality – particularly in the presence of TV cameras – those days are gone. The current reality of the Australian market is **computerised trading**.

'Open outcry' equity trading floors were replaced by a national **computerised trading system** in **1990** and since then all ASX-listed shares have been traded electronically on the **Stock Exchange Automated Trading System (SEATS)**. After you lodge your buy or sell order over the phone, or via your on-line broker, it is sent to, accepted and executed on **SEATS**. Orders are actively traded on the market between **10am and 4pm** from **Monday to Friday**.

Only **ASX clearing members** (stockbrokers and financial advisors with Australian Financial Services Licences authorising them to deal in securities) have access to SEATS. When you place an order with your broker, a licensed SEATs operator enters it into the system via a specialised terminal in the office. All orders are queued according to **time and price priority**. It's a case of 'first in, best dressed', regardless of order size, with the best (highest) bid going to the top of the buyers' queue to wait for a seller and the best (lowest) offer going to the top of the sellers' queue to wait for a buyer. It's a highly dynamic queue and trades are executed automatically in order of time/price priority by matching buying and selling orders in the system. While computerised trading lacks the 'colour' and atmosphere of floor trading, the system is designed to provide more **equal market access** and a more **efficient trading platform** for both large and small investors.

Orders remain in the system until the transaction is **completed or cancelled**, although orders that are a long way out of the market are routinely purged from the system. You can also **amend** all or part of your order – price and/or quantity – until it is executed. If you are trading on-line, your order might be relayed to your broker's office and entered into the system by a **SEATS operator**. As mentioned earlier, some brokers offer **straight through order processing**, which eliminates the delays that can be caused by double handling as orders are sent directly into SEATS – usually within a matter of seconds.

GEARING INTO THE SHARE MARKET

Borrowing money – or **gearing** – by taking out a **margin or equity loan** are ways in which you can maximise your potential returns by boosting your investment power. **Gearing** works on the principle that if your investment returns are greater than your interest repayments, you'll come out in front. However, there are **risks** associated with this strategy, and you should be aware of these before considering signing on the dotted line.

Margin lending

There has been a rapid growth in the popularity of **margin lending products**. This growth was partly fuelled by the influx of investors looking for more leverage to participate in the 'bull run' that stampeded across the stock market at various times during the 1990s. Even though market conditions in 2002 are very different – and the boom has given way to a more jittery market – demand for margin loans still appears to be relatively strong.

Investment advisors point out that margin lending is better suited to investors who have a reasonably **high tolerance to risk** coupled with a reasonably **high and reliable income** who are planning to invest for the **medium to long term**. Ideally you should have a **good grasp** of the stock market as well as the willingness to take on **greater risk** for the prospect of higher returns. It's really important to be aware that while margin lending can **exponentially magnify your returns**, on the downside it can also substantially **magnify losses** should the value of your share portfolio nosedive. In other words, it's not right for everyone and novice investors tend to be more at risk of falling victim to the dreaded margin call. Before you even consider gearing into the market via a margin loan, **learn how margin lending works** and understand its risks. You should also be confident that you have sufficient funds to meet the interest payments on the loan to avoid defaulting.

How does it work?

In a nutshell, a margin loan allows you to leverage into the market by **borrowing funds to buy more shares** than would typically be possible by relying on your own funds. In this way you can really beef up your portfolio while the underlying shares secure the borrowed funds. While you will generally be required to contribute **some of your own money**, margin lending allows you to build a substantial share portfolio with as little as a 30% (and sometimes 20%) **deposit**. Margin lenders will usually permit you to borrow between **30% and 70%** of the market value of your investments.

It is possible to borrow money directly against your existing shares to top up your portfolio even further. A margin loan can provide the means to increase both the **size and diversity** of your share portfolio – potentially giving your investment returns a major shot in the arm.

Margin calls

Buying shares through a margin loan, however, heightens your **exposure to the market** and **amplifies** the impact of **its peaks and troughs** on the value your shareholdings. Furthermore, the accepted **trade-off** for the prospect of higher rewards is that you run the risk of a **'margin call'** if the market value of your portfolio falls and starts approaching the value of your loan. Margin calls can rear their heads when there is a major drop in the value of your shares or when the market as a whole is falling.

Your lender makes the unwelcome 'call' and you will then have to:

- ◆ **produce additional funds** to reduce the borrowed amount
- ◆ raise money by **selling** off some of your shares
- ◆ boost the value of your portfolio by purchasing **additional shares**.

If you have taken out a margin loan you have to accept that encountering a margin call at some stage is a real possibility. Investment advisors strongly recommend that you have **accessible cash** or **extra security** on hand at all times. You usually only have a 24-hour window period to respond to a margin call. If your investment strategy goes totally pear-shaped – and you are forced to default on the loan – the lender is entitled to **sell your shares at a loss** to cover the margin call.

Avoiding margin lending pitfalls

You can reduce the chance of a margin call by treading somewhat **cautiously** and not using all the available funds at your disposable. For example, if you borrow 50% instead of 70% of a portfolio's value, its value would have to fall by about one-third before encountering a margin call. On the other hand, your portfolio's value would have to fall by less than one-tenth to put you in line for a margin call if you had borrowed the full 70%.

By **diversifying** your portfolio across different sectors you can minimise the impact of market fluctuations on the value of your shareholdings. You can also erect **additional safety nets** by keeping up-to-date on interest payments and carefully monitoring your portfolio and rebalancing it if necessary. Given that margin lending does carry a high level of risk, investment professionals recommend seeking **independent advice** to closely examine the terms and conditions of the loan – and to determine whether margin lending is the most appropriate strategy for you.

Equity loans

Increasing numbers of **home owners** are unlocking the equity in their home in the form of a **loan** to finance investments like shares. An equity loan allows you to take advantage of your property's built-up value now, instead of waiting until it's sold to get your hands on the cash. With equity loans it is possible to borrow up to 90% of the value of your home.

How do they work?

If property prices are booming, you may be sitting on – or living in – an untapped reservoir of wealth. Dipping into this reservoir by taking out a home equity loan can be a good way to put your **stored equity** to work via leverage into the share market. As with margin loans, these borrowed funds can help you to maximise your investment returns by allowing you to buy more shares and to diversify your portfolio to multiply your investment returns. As well as giving you the means to buy an asset class that is likely to experience capital growth, the dividends earned from shares can also help to pay off your home mortgage more quickly. However, you should avoid diving into the gearing deep end without doing your homework or seeking independent advice to make sure that an equity loan is the right strategy for you.

Negative gearing

Negative gearing is made possible when the **income from your shares is less than the cost of your investment** – in other words, the interest on the loan and brokerage costs. The difference between the two amounts can generally be claimed as a **deduction** on your taxable income. It's important to remember that these deductions are pointless unless your share portfolio rises in value. Investment professionals advise that the tax breaks offered by negative gearing should be treated as a bonus and that your overriding concern should be investing for profit rather than reducing tax liability.

You should not consider negative gearing unless you are confident of meeting the **interest payments** – even if the market falls and the value of your shares was to flounder for a period of time.

Negative gearing is not for all investors. It is more suitable for those in the highest income tax bracket, so you can take full advantage of the tax deductibility of your interest payments to reduce the actual cost of the borrowed money.

Avoiding the pitfalls

Like margin lending, investment advisors warn against fully gearing into the share market with an equity loan because the flipside of **multiplying**

your returns is that you can also **magnify your losses**. Therefore it's a good idea to borrow **less** than the maximum allowable amount. As shares are a risky investment in the short to medium term, don't borrow against your house if you are not confident about your **job security** or if you don't have **cash reserves**. You will still be obligated to meet interest repayments if the value of your shareholding falls. Another thing to keep in mind is your capacity to repay the loan if **interest rates rise**.

A home equity loan can also lead to a **reduction in the principal equity** in your home. For example, if the value of your shares declines significantly, you could be staring down the barrel of a struggling share portfolio and diminished equity in your property. The worst-case scenario is that you could **lose your home** if you are heavily geared and the stock market collapses. It is generally recommended that only savvy investors with a firm grasp of the share market and an understanding of the risks involved should use the equity in their home to invest in shares. Finally, as with margin loans, understanding the **terms and conditions** associated with the lending product are vitally important.

TAX: FACING THE INEVITABLE

As with most investments, your home being the exception, the Australian Tax Office (ATO) will take its 'due'. You will be required to pay **capital gains tax (CGT)** on profits realised from the sale of your share holdings. On a brighter note, **losses** sustained when disposing of your shares can be **offset** against profits, and **brokerage fees** are **tax deductible**.

Capital gains tax applies to any **capital profit** made on **selling shares** and most other investments. If you incurred a **capital loss** when you sold your shares, it can be claimed against other capital gains made in that financial year, or it can be carried forward and offset against **future capital gains** from shares or other assets. It's important to note that this offset **doesn't apply** to other forms of taxable income.

How does CGT work?

Only shares purchased **on or after 20 September 1985** are subject to CGT. The profit is calculated after taking into account all costs of buying and selling, as well as adjustment for inflation. CGT is only levied when your **shares are sold** and the tax payable is determined by your marginal tax rate in that particular financial year to 30 June.

For shares bought **after 21 September 1999**, the **new CGT system** applies. If you sell your shares **12 months or more** after the date that you purchased them, CGT is charged on the gain at only half your highest marginal rate. For example, if you are in the highest tax bracket of 48.5%, the tax will be levied at 24.25%. If they were held for **less than 12 months**, this concession doesn't apply and the full value of the capital gain will be incorporated into your taxable income. With shares purchased **prior to 21 September 1999**, you can choose to take advantage of these CGT rules or you can elect to go with the **inflation-indexed rules** of the preceding system. Under the new CGT system there is no inflation allowance as there is in the previous CGT regime.

More information

This is a **general outline** of the key points in relation to CGT and is not intended to be a definitive guide. As the issue of taxation is a specialised and multifaceted one, there isn't sufficient space to cover it completely in this book. To find out more about calculating your CGT liability, refer to the Australian Tax Office website at www.ato.gov.au or call 13 28 61 for more information. Alternately, it may be worthwhile discussing CGT liability with an accountant who can also advise you on managing these liabilities.

MANAGED SHARE FUNDS

It goes without saying that in order to become a smart and successful share market investor you have to be prepared to spend time and work hard to build and manage your portfolio. If you are interested in investing in shares but the processes involved seem too onerous or time-consuming, then a **managed share fund** might be the way to go.

What is a managed share fund?

In brief, when you buy units in a managed share fund, your money is **pooled** with that of many other investors and it is managed as one big share portfolio. **Professional fund managers** select the shares and administer the investment. You and the other investors share the profits from any appreciation in the fund's value, and the losses if it falls.

Managed share funds employ two main investment strategies. **Index funds** are based on a long-term **'buy-and-hold' strategy** and they seek to generate returns in line with the performance of a market index, like the All Ordinaries, for example. **Active funds**, on the other hand, tend to take a shorter-term approach and actively **select specific shares** in an effort to beat benchmark market indexes whilst outperforming competing funds.

What do they offer?

An extensive range of managed share funds is available to Australian investors across a range of companies and sectors. Some managed share funds focus only on **Australian shares** or a **specific area of the market** (eg. the Resources sector) or small emerging companies. Others offer a **mixture** of these. It's even possible to buy into **specialty funds** like ethical investments or a fund consisting only of fully franked Australian shares. You can also invest in **international share funds** across a variety of countries within a specific region, like Western Europe or South-East Asia, or particular international markets like the USA, or even a combination of regions and markets.

Managed funds vs direct investing

There is probably room to include both **managed share funds** and **direct share investing** into your investment strategy, and both methods have their pros and cons.

Diversification

Managed funds are a great way to **diversify** your share portfolio with only a small initial minimum outlay of $1000 followed by a

$100 investment every month. By pooling funds with other investors you can share in the returns of **numerous companies** in an Australian share fund and **dozens of markets** internationally. If you were buying shares directly, and didn't have large sums of money to invest, this level of diversification might be beyond your reach. Consequently, a managed share fund enables you to potentially achieve better returns than if you invested directly in a handful of companies in a single country.

The trade-off with diversification through a fund is that this type of investment can **limit your potential** for the type of gain you might see if you owned shares in a single company that recorded a massive increase in value. (The arguments for diversification, however, would certainly outweigh those in favour of the **risky strategy** of owning a single stock and hoping for this scenario.) You cannot count on skyrocketing values and, if they do occur, share prices can come back to earth with a thud, leaving a big dent in your investment capital. This situation was evidenced during the 'tech boom' of the late 90s and subsequent 'bust' of 2000.

Risk

You can also **reduce your risk** via a managed share fund. However, even professionally managed investments **cannot completely eliminate** your risk of losing some money at some time. Managed investments don't come with a built-in guarantee – their yields can fluctuate and the value of share funds can fall in value. Therefore, while investing in a managed fund frees you from the risk of selecting your own shares, selecting the 'right' **fund manager** means that you take on board another type of risk.

When it comes to choosing a share fund, as with direct share investments, it's a good idea to adopt a **longer-term strategy**, as funds aren't insulated from rises and falls in the market. Investment advisors recommend that you analyse a fund manager's **investment approach and style** and then decide if the **objectives** of the fund match your investment requirements. They also recommend that you look beyond just the previous year's performance and take into account the **five and 10-year performances** of the fund. However, they also point out that past returns are not necessarily a reliable guide of future performance.

Control

When buying shares directly, *you* **decide** which of the roughly 1450 companies trading on the ASX across 24 sectors you want to add to your portfolio. **Researching** companies and keeping abreast of market movements requires some time and effort. However, it lets you play an **active role** in identifying buying and selling opportunities and monitoring

the performance of your shares. Investing in a managed fund **doesn't allow you** to exercise this level of control and choice but an experienced manager aims to ensure that the ongoing share investments remain consistent with the fund's goal of providing **solid returns** over time.

Cost

When you buy and sell shares directly you will have to pay **brokerage** on each transaction. However, there are no ongoing costs. Managed funds can be a convenient and profitable way of investing in the share market, but **professional management comes at a cost**. In order to pay the highly qualified professionals who conduct ongoing research and monitor your investments, the funds charge a **management fee (MER)** of around **1–2%** each year. You could also be up for **sales commissions** and fund managers usually charge **entry and exit fees** of 1.5–4% of the investment's value. The worst-kept secret in the industry is that you can avoid entry fees by joining a fund **via some discount brokers**. Some will rebate 100% of the entry fees charged by the respective fund managers. You should carefully **examine all costs** involved before investing in a managed fund. For example, actively managed funds tend to have higher operating costs than indexed funds because they buy and sell shares **aggressively** to try and outperform the market index. Be aware that fees can **vary widely** from fund to fund.

Researching managed share funds

Do your homework before deciding on which managed fund is the right one for you. There are good sources of information for researching managed funds. Several **websites** provide useful information, including **types of funds** on offer and contact details of the various funds managers. Some also offer **comparisons, ratings and analysis** of various funds. Many of the websites listed in on page 18 provide excellent information on managed funds, but there are also several valuable **specialist sites** available, such as www.assirt.com.au, www.morningstar.com.au, www.investorweb.com.au and www.facs.gov.au/invest/IM_index.htm. *Shares*, *Personal Investor* and *Money Magazine*, the *Australian Financial Review* and the finance pages of the major dailies also feature write-ups about managed funds. Finally, you can obtain information directly **over the phone** from the fund managers and have information sent out to you. Alternately, you can **download prospectuses** from their websites. **Stockbrokers** acting as entry points into managed funds also offer on-line and hard-copy prospectuses.

GLOSSARY

All Ordinaries Index The index measuring the market prices of the major stocks with the highest market turnover listed on the Australian Stock Exchange (ASX).

Annual General Meeting (AGM) A company's yearly meeting of directors and shareholders covering issues such as approval of the previous year's financial results, discussion of shareholder resolutions and the election of directors.

Asset class A group of financial assets, such as shares, cash, fixed interest or property.

Australian Financial Services Licence (AFSL) A licence issued by the Australian Securities and Investments Commission (ASIC) under the *Corporations Law* (as amended by the *Financial Services Reform Act* 2002).

Australian Securities and Investment Commission (ASIC) A government regulatory body established in 1991 (and renamed in 1998) to administer and enforce the *Corporations Law* and consumer law to protect investors.

Australian Stock Exchange (ASX) The national organisation that facilitates the trading of Australian equities and derivatives. It replaced the individual State-based stock exchanges in 1987.

Average price The mean (average) price achieved when buying or selling a parcel of shares.

Balance sheet A financial statement that demonstrates both the amount and type of assets, liabilities and capital a company has on a particular date.

Blue-chip A popular and accepted term to describe quality shares in large, established, well-managed companies with a solid track record and profitability over a long period of time.

Bond A fixed interest investment issued by governments or companies.

Bonus issue Shares issued to existing shareholders based on the proportion of existing shareholdings. They are funded from the issuing company's reserves at no cost to the investor.

Brokerage The fee charged by a stockbroker for executing buy and sell transactions. Brokerage fees are charged according to a scale based on the total value of shares traded or a percentage of the total value of the transaction.

Capital gain/loss The difference between the cost and selling price of a parcel of shares.

Capital gains tax (CGT) A tax imposed on the capital profit from the sale of shares (or other investments) acquired after 20 September 1985. It is adjusted for inflation and only levied when the capital gain is realised. Capital

losses can also be offset against other taxation liabilities in some cases. A new regime became effective from 21 September 1999 and adjustment for inflation does not apply to shares purchased from this date.

Capital growth The increase in the market value of shares (or other investments) over a period of time.

Cash One of the main asset classes. Low risk investments (eg. cash management trusts and term deposits) that are easily redeemable.

Cash flow The net amount of cash received over a period of time in relation to a company's accounts.

Cash management trust (CMT) Unit trust which enables the pooling of large numbers of investors' funds. Higher returns can be achieved by pooling funds that might not otherwise be available to individual investors. They are highly liquid and more flexible than fixed-rate term deposits.

Chaikin Money Flow Oscillator It works on the basis of tracking buying pressure (when a stock closes in the upper half of a period's range) and selling pressure (when a stock closes in the lower half of the period's trading range).

Clearing House Electronic Subregister System (CHESS) The electronic transfer and settlement system for share transactions – the Australian Stock Exchange (ASX) introduced it in 1994.

Company A legal entity regulated by the Australian Securities Commission under the *Corporations Law*.

Contributing shares Shares that are not fully paid.

Corporations Law A series of Acts passed by the Australian Parliament to regulate the operation of Australian companies and the securities and futures markets.

Currency A country's unit of exchange (eg. the Australian dollar, the US dollar, the Japanese yen and the Euro).

Currency risk The risk of loss in the value of an overseas investment due to movements in international exchange rates.

Director An individual elected by shareholders who assumes the responsibility for overseeing the operation and management of a company.

Diversification Spreading funds across various sectors and markets in order to spread out and manage risk.

Dividend The amount of after-tax earnings paid to company shareholders. Dividends can be fully or partly franked.

Dividend imputation Avoids the double taxing on the dividends of shares by giving investors in companies that pay the Australian corporate tax rate credits for tax paid on corporate profits. Excess franking credits may be claimed as a tax refund on an individual's tax returns.

Dividend yield The actual return on an investment calculated by dividing the dividend rate by the current share price of a company and expressing the result as a percentage.

Dow Jones New York's 'Dow Jones Industrial Average' which measures the average share price of a group of 30 major companies actively traded on the New York Stock Exchange.

Earnings per share (EPS) A measure of a company's performance calculated by dividing the company's after-tax net operating profit by the number of shares issued.

Earnings yield A ratio calculated by dividing a company's earnings per share by its current share price.

Emerging markets Financial markets in countries with 'developing economies' like South-East Asia and Latin America. These types of markets offer potentially high returns along with higher volatility and risk.

Entry fee A fee or commission charged when an investor joins (or enters) some pooled investments (eg. managed funds).

Equity The actual 'share' and/or the value an investor holds in an asset.

Ethical investment An investment strategy with a 'social conscience' that extends beyond the potential for financial returns. For example, an ethical investment approach may exclude specific sectors like tobacco or some mining companies and lean towards investments in companies that are environmentally conscious.

Exit fee A fee charged by some pooled investments when an investor redeems units (withdraws funds).

Exponential moving average (EMA) Exponential moving averages are calculated by applying a percentage of today's closing price to yesterday's moving average value.

Fixed interest An asset class that provides a fixed level of income that does not fluctuate over the investment timeframe (eg. bonds).

Float The decision by a company to offer its shares to the public. Also known as an initial public offering (IPO).

Franked dividends Dividends on shares in Australian companies with imputation credits attached. A franking credit is available to shareholders in order to avoid a double tax on the company's profit. Depending on the amount of tax already paid by the company, a percentage of up to 100% of a dividend may be franked. Dividends are fully franked when a company pays the full company tax rate.

FTSE The Financial Times Stock Exchange Index (FTSE) is the UK equivalent of the Australian All Ordinaries Index. It lists the 100 largest public companies trading on the London Stock Exchange.

Fundamental analysis Analysis of share values based on quantitative and qualitative factors, including earnings forecasts and company management. These factors take current share prices into consideration to determine if the shares have been mispriced, undervalued or overvalued.

Fund manager An organisation that invests in a portfolio of assets (eg. a managed fund) on behalf of individuals and/or organisations. Pooled funds are managed according to a particular investment style on a day-to-day basis and are based on the requirements of the investors.

Gearing Increasing exposure to the market by borrowing (eg. margin or equity loan) to multiply potential returns. This can also multiply investment losses.

Growth assets Includes asset classes like shares and property that offer capital growth and income over a period of time and can be expected to outpace inflation.

Imputation credit Taxation credits received by shareholders who have received franked dividends from their shareholdings in a company.

Income stream The money earned from investments (eg. dividends from shares).

Inflation The increase of prices of goods and services in the economy.

Initial public offering (IPO) See *Float*

Investment An asset purchased by an investor with a view to producing capital growth/gains and/or income.

Investment manager See *Fund manager*

Last sale The last price at which a stock was traded on a particular day, or time, during an ASX trading session.

Liabilities Debts (also, the dividends to be paid to shareholders).

Limit order An order to buy or sell a specified number of ASX-listed shares at a specified, or better, price.

Listed Property Trust A portfolio of a range of properties listed on the ASX and owned by a pool of investors, ensuring a broader spread of property ownership than what would be available to most individual investors.

Liquidity The capacity to convert an investment into cash quickly without the risk of losing a big portion of capital outlay.

Managed funds Managed funds are the pooled investments of a large number of investors under the control of a professional fund manager. Investments can be spread across a range of investment options. The fund manager makes the investment decisions and charges a management fee. All the investors in that particular fund share profits or losses.

Margin call A requirement that the client of a broker tops up his or her margin loans to the required minimum level in order to cover a fall in the value of an investment portfolio due to adverse market movements.

Marketable parcel The minimum allowable number of shares in a listed stock that can be traded on the ASX.

Market cycle Measured by an index and relates to fluctuations in market activity. Typically, market cycles match up with prevailing economic conditions involving strong buying activity (suggesting growth) and heavy stock sell-off (suggesting a downturn).

Market order An order to buy or sell shares in an ASX-listed stock at the best price available at the time of receipt into SEATS.

Market price The highest price that a buyer is prepared to pay and the lowest price a seller is willing to accept without the obligation to execute at those prices. It can also be the last price at which a share is sold.

Market risk Risk relating to the market as a whole which cannot be managed by portfolio diversification.

Merger Corporate restructuring negotiated by the management of the companies and involving the joining of two companies into one.

Moving averages Moving averages show the average value of a share's price over a period of time.

Negative gearing The purchase of an investment using borrowed funds where the interest on the borrowing (and other costs) exceeds the income from that investment. Generally, the negative net income can be offset against other income for tax purposes.

Non-renounceable rights Rights associated with a share that cannot be traded on the market.

Ordinary shares Shares that represent ownership in a listed company and entitle shareholders to a share in that company's profits.

Over-subscribed When the interest in an IPO (float) is so great that the number of or value of applications received for the new share issue exceeds the amount of shares available for allocation.

Paper profits See *Unrealised profits*

Portfolio The pool of investments held by an investor, ie. the combination of shares in different companies, sectors and markets or across the asset classes of securities, like property, cash, fixed interest and shares.

Preference shares Shares that usually provide a fixed rate of return on the 'unfranked' investment. Preference shareholders are given preferential treatment over ordinary shareholders in the issuing of dividends. They also outrank ordinary shares if a company collapses.

Price to earnings ratio (P/E ratio) The current market price of a share divided by the estimated future earnings per share. It is one of the most common fundamental analysis tools and a high P/E ratio suggests that the market has high expectations of growth and profit.

Profit and loss account A financial statement revealing company expenses and earnings over a particular period of time.

Prospectus A document providing detailed information to potential investors in a financial product (eg. float) lodged with ASIC. Companies seeking to raise capital from the public by listing on the ASX must provide sufficient information in the prospectus to enable investors to make an informed decision.

Rate of return The income yield earned in relation to the amount of capital invested.

Registry Organisation engaged to issue shares authorised by a company.

Relative strength index (RSI) An indicator that compares the days that a stock finishes up higher against when it finishes lower.

Return The amount of money, usually expressed as a percentage, received from an investment annually.

Rights issue An offer to purchase new shares issued by a company (at a discount to the current market price) made available to existing shareholders in that company.

Risk Risk pertains to the uncertainty of investment returns. In line with the 'risk = reward' axiom, investments with higher levels of risk should be expected to deliver higher potential returns to compensate for a greater possibility of losing a portion (or even the full amount) of initial capital outlay. Risk can include market risk, investor risk, company risk, portfolio risk and currency risk.

SEATS The Stock Exchange Automated Trading System.

Sector A group of securities operating in the same type of industry and sharing common characteristics (eg. the Banking and Finance, Media, Telecommunications and Resources sectors).

Sell order Order issued to a stockbroker authorising the sale of a specified quantity of shares.

Settlement An arrangement between stockbroking firms and the buyer/seller for the payment of transactions in securities like shares. It is conducted by the ASX stock clearing system (CHESS) and is the final stage of a share transaction and the delivery of shares. See also *Clearing House Electronic Sub-register System (CHESS)*.

Share The part-ownership of a company. A shareholder has an interest in the management of the company, the right to a share of the profits and a claim on remaining assets (following the payment of creditors) if a company collapses.

Share Price Index An index measuring the broad movements in the prices of shares.

Share register A register recording all of a company's shareholders and the number of shares held by each one.

Smaller companies A term usually applied to companies listed outside the top 100 shares on the stock exchange.

Speculative investments High-risk investments where there is a higher risk of losing some or all of capital outlay.

Standard & Poor's (S&P) The United States credit rating agency which provides the basis on which indexes are calculated.

Stock Another term for shares or equities.

Stockbroker An ASX Clearing Member licensed by ASIC (ie. a holder of an Australian Financial Services Licence) who is authorised to buy and sell shares on behalf of investors who pay brokerage fees on the transaction.

Takeover The acquisition of shares in one company by another in order to secure a controlling interest in that company.

Tax deduction An expense that can be offset (deducted) against tax liabilities.

Tax File Number (TFN) A number issued to taxpayers by the Australian Taxation Office (ATO). The ATO uses TFNs to match income and taxation details of taxpayers.

Technical analysis A form of stock analysis that focuses on the technical elements of market activity. In contrast to fundamental analysis, this approach relies heavily on charts. It examines patterns of price change and uses indicators like resistance, momentum and support in an attempt to predict future trends.

Time horizon The set period of time over which an investor plans to realise his or her stated investment objectives.

Trader An individual who actively buys and sells shares for his or her personal account, usually within a relatively short space of time. It is a high-risk market strategy that can deliver higher-than-average returns but can also lead to heavy losses.

Turnover The level of trading (trading activity and volumes) that occur in the market.

Qualitative analysis Valuing companies based on subjective elements such as management, economic factors, corporate strategy and outlook.

Quantitative analysis Valuing of companies using objective, numerical factors, such as P/E ratios, earnings per share, yield and price momentum.

Unfranked dividends Dividends paid to shareholders by companies that are not subject to Australian tax. Unfranked dividends are taxed at their normal marginal rate.

Unrealised profits Profits that have not been taken, as the shareholder has not sold the stock even though the price has increased. Also known as 'paper profits'.

Value investor An investor whose investment strategy involves buying shares when they appear to be undervalued with a view to making a profit when they look as if they are overvalued.

Volatility The degree to which a share price rises and falls – a measure of risk.

INDEX